Rio Ferdinand

Andy Croft

Published in association with The Basic Skills Agency

Hodder Murray
A MEMBER OF THE HODDER HEADLINE GROUP

The Publishers would like to thank the following for permission to reproduce copyright material:

Photo credits
p.3 © Brian Rasic/Rex Features; p.8 © John Marsh/Empics; p.13 © Tony Marshall/Empics; pp.18, 23 © Neal Simpson/Empics; p.21 © Alex Livesey/Getty Images; p.25 © Rex Features; p.27 © Rebecca Naden/PA/Empics.

Orders: please contact Bookpoint Ltd, 130 Milton Park, Abingdon, Oxon OX14 4SB. Telephone (44) 01235 827720. Fax: (44) 01235 400454. Lines are open from 9.00–6.00, Monday to Saturday, with a 24-hour message answering service. You can also order through our website www.hoddereducation.co.uk

© Andy Croft 2003, 2005
Second Edition. First published in 2003 by
Hodder Murray, a member of the Hodder Headline Group
338 Euston Road
London NW1 3BH

Impression number 10 9 8 7 6 5 4 3 2 1
Year   2010 2009 2008 2007 2006 2005

Cover photo © Matthew Peters/Manchester United via Getty Images
Typeset in 14pt Palatino by SX Composing DTP, Rayleigh, Essex.
Printed in Great Britain by CPI Bath.

A catalogue record for this title is available from the British Library

ISBN-10 0 340 90076 8
ISBN-13 978 0 340 90076 5

Contents

1 Beginnings

Rio Gavin Ferdinand
was born on 8 November 1978
in Dulwich
in South-East London.

He was the eldest of four children.
One of his cousins is
Spurs and England player Les Ferdinand.

Rio's parents split up when he was 12.
Rio was brought up by his Mum.
They lived on the Friary Estate in Peckham.
It was a tough area. It still is.

Especially if you don't have much money.
Especially if you are black.
Rio was at school with Stephen Lawrence,
the black teenager killed by racists.
Not long ago a schoolboy called Damilola Taylor
was stabbed to death near Rio's old house.

Rio went to Camelot Primary School
and Blackheath Bluecoats Secondary School.
His favourite subject was Drama.
He liked acting in plays and singing in musicals.
He was good at PE, athletics, swimming
and football.
He was also good at Maths.
He liked reading.
His favourite writer was Roald Dahl,
especially *The Twits*.

When he was young Rio supported Liverpool.
His favourite footballer was
Liverpool and England striker John Barnes.
His other heroes were Mike Tyson
and Diego Maradona.

Rio Ferdinand.

He joined a local junior football team
called Bloomfields.
He played centre-forward
and once scored 30 goals in a season.

When Rio was 12 he joined Eltham Town.
He played in midfield
for the Under-13 and Under-14 teams.

2 West Ham

Rio was spotted by West Ham scouts
playing for Eltham when he was 14.
He signed on for West Ham as a schoolboy.
When he was 16,
he was signed as an apprentice at Upton Park.
Lots of other clubs wanted to sign Rio Ferdinand.
But Rio was happy playing for the Hammers.

He only earned £30 a week.
One of his jobs was cleaning the boots
for manager Harry Redknapp.
He wasn't very good at it!

When he was 17
he became a professional.
He bought his Mum a new house.
When he wasn't training,
he studied Sports Science at college.

Rio played in the West Ham Youth team.
In 1996 they won
the South-East Counties championship
and reached the FA Youth Cup final.
Soon he was playing for West Ham Reserves.

Harry Redknapp wanted to give Rio
more first-team experience.
In 1996 Rio went on loan to Bournemouth.
He played ten games for the team.
Bournemouth fans still remember young Rio
playing at Dean Court.

In May 1996 Rio played for West Ham first team.
He came on as second-half substitute
against Sheffield Wednesday.

In January 1997 he played
his first full game for West Ham,
against Wrexham in the FA Cup.
In February 1997 he scored his first goal
for the Hammers, against Blackburn.
In his first full season at Upton Park
Rio played 16 games.

By the next season Rio was a first team regular.
He played 45 times.
In five seasons Rio played 152 games for West Ham.

Rio celebrates a goal with West Ham.

3 A Rolls Royce

Rio Ferdinand is a great athlete.

He is strong.

He is fast.

He is 6 foot 3 inches (188 cm) tall.

He weighs 13 st 8 lbs (12.1 kg).

He has good pace.

He has stamina.

He is good in the air.

He never panics.

He organises the defence.

He reads the game well.

He likes to put his foot on the ball.

He doesn't play his team-mates into trouble.

He can move out of defence with the ball.

'He's a real special player,'
said Harry Redknapp,
just like 'a Rolls Royce'.

West Ham fans loved Rio.
They have always liked
skilful players at West Ham.
They voted him 'Hammer of the Year' in 1998.
Some fans said
he was almost as good
as the great Bobby Moore.

4 England

It wasn't long before England fans
wanted Rio Ferdinand
to play for his country.

In 1997, he played for the England Under-21 team
against Sweden and Germany.
He played three more times for the Under-21 team,
against Italy, Greece and Yugoslavia.

Rio won his first full cap
in November 1998
against Cameroon at Wembley.

But he didn't get much of a chance
under England managers
Glen Hoddle and Kevin Keegan.

He was in the 1998 World Cup squad
but he didn't play a single game.

Rio at the World Cup.

5 Leeds United

By now a lot of clubs
wanted to buy Rio Ferdinand.
Rio was happy at West Ham.
But he wanted to win something.
Barcelona and Real Madrid
wanted to buy him.
But Rio wanted to play in England.

In November 2000
Leeds United paid £18 million for Rio.
It was the British transfer record.
Some people said it was too much money.
But manager David O'Leary
knew Rio was worth every penny.
He made him club captain.

Rio played 32 games
in his first season at Elland Road.
He helped Leeds reach
the semi-finals of the Champions' League.
He scored his first goal for Leeds
in the Champions' League quarter-final.
The next week he scored against Liverpool.
The following week
he scored against West Ham.
The West Ham fans cheered him!

In the next two seasons
Rio played 73 games for Leeds.

6 World Cup 2002

In 2001, Sven Goran Eriksson
became England manager.
He wanted to win the World Cup.

Sven made Rio
and Sol Campbell
his first choices at the back.
They are two of the best
centre-backs in the world.
They are both big and fast,
strong and skilful.

With Rio and Sol Campbell at the back,
England beat Finland, Albania and Greece.
Then came the biggest test of Rio's life.
England against Germany.
Germany had never lost a World Cup game at home.
Everyone thought Germany would win.
Germany scored after a few minutes.
England fans thought the game was over.

But not the England players.
Not Rio Ferdinand.
They fought back.
Rio made every tackle count.
The German players couldn't get past him.
Michael Owen scored.
Steven Gerrard put England ahead.
In the end it was easy.
England 5, Germany 1!

England 5 : 1 Germany!

England drew with Sweden and Nigeria.
Then they beat Argentina 1–0.
It was Rio's best game in an England shirt.
He was like a rock in the middle of the field.
The Argentinians tried everything.
But Rio stood firm.
In the next game
Rio headed in a David Beckham cross.
England 3, Denmark 0.
It was his first England goal.
Rio had another great game against Brazil.
But not even Rio Ferdinand
could stop the Brazilians.

England were knocked out.
But Rio Ferdinand
was now world famous.

7 Manchester United

In June 2002, Leeds sacked David O'Leary.
Leeds were short of money.
So then Leeds sold Rio to Manchester United
for £30 million.
It is a British record.
It is a world record price for a defender.
The boy from Peckham
is now the most valuable defender in the world.
Some people said it was too much money.
But Alex Ferguson knows Rio is worth it.
'He will be the best,' he says.

Manchester United sign Rio, July 2002.

In his first season Rio helped Manchester United
to win the League.

But then he forgot to go for a drugs test.
The FA banned him from playing
for eight months.

United missed him.
England missed him.
The fans missed him.

But Rio trained hard.
He couldn't wait to play again

When he came back
at the start of the 2003–4 season,
he was even sharper and stronger than ever.
Rio made his return at a match with Liverpool.
Manchester United won 2–1.

Rio playing for Manchester United.

8 The Beckham from Peckham

Rio Ferdinand has come a long way
from the estate in Peckham
where he grew up.
He plays for the biggest club in the world.
He plays in one of the best teams in the world.
At one of the best grounds in the world.
In front of one of the biggest crowds in the world.
And he is still only 26.

He earns £60,000 a week.
He goes on holiday to Cyprus.
He drives an Aston Martin.
His crooked smile is very famous.

Rio in London, 2002.

But he hasn't really changed much.
His favourite foods are Italian and Caribbean
(and anything cooked by his Mum or his Nan).
He relaxes by playing tennis and table-tennis
and watching basketball.
His favourite basketball player is Michael Jordan.
Rio still likes reading.
He always takes a book to read
when he is travelling to away games.

He still gets angry about racist football fans.
He supports Kick Racism Out of Football.

The England football team supports 'Kick Racism Out of Football' before training at Arsenal's ground.

27

Perhaps one day Rio Ferdinand
will be captain of Manchester United.
Perhaps one day he will be
captain of England.
Perhaps one day he will
help England win the World Cup.